BURTON & ASHBY TRAMWAYS

Peter M White

Series editor Robert J Harley

MP Middleton Press

Cover picture: There are many photographs of grossly overloaded cars running in convoy, carrying group outings. A rare high quality picture shows the Swadlincote United Methodist Free Church School Treat on 9th June 1908.

Cover colours: Only the red is of relevance: it represents the Midland Railway red used on the main panels.

```
┌─────────────────────────────────────────────────────────┐
│                                                           │
│   Dedicated to my good  friend the late J.W.Storer        │
│                                                           │
└─────────────────────────────────────────────────────────┘
```

First published October 2000

ISBN 1 901706 51 6

© Middleton Press, 2000

Design David Pede

Published by
   Middleton Press
   Easebourne Lane
   Midhurst, West Sussex
   GU29 9AZ
Tel: 01730 813169
Fax: 01730 812601

Printed & bound by Biddles Ltd,
   Guildford and Kings Lynn

CONTENTS

ACKNOWLEDGMENTS

Sincere appreciation is due to K.Gilliver for his insight into the history of Breweries and P.Swift for giving us the benefit of his knowledge of technical details, also many local inhabitants of South Derbyshire. Photographs have been contributed by the Burton Mail, Mark Bown, British Rail, Richard Farman and J.S.Simnett and my thanks go to them. Others are included from my own collection. The tickets have been provided by Godfrey Croughton and Glynn Waite. Route map by Mike Pearson and is included with his kind permission.

FOREWORD

Peter White has kindly asked me to write a foreword to this book. My only qualification for this honour is that, when I saw Peter sitting next to Mr Middleton Press (Vic Mitchell) at the Model Tramways Exhibition at Kew Bridge Steam Museum in July 1999, I thought that it might be productive to introduce them to each other.

The text of this book is based on *Sixpenny Switchback*, written by Peter White and Joe Storer in 1983, and published locally in Burton. *Sixpenny Switchback* has been long out of print, so a book dealing with the narrow gauge tramways which served Burton-on-Trent and the group of small industrial towns and villages between Burton and Ashby is well overdue.

Sadly, Joe Storer died a few years ago, so will not see this new version of his book, which is illustrated by some of Peter White's vast collection of old photographs of the Burton - Swadlincote - Ashby area. Peter and Joe, together with other members of the Gresley Group, were instrumental in rescuing and rebuilding the body of Burton & Ashby Car 14. This went to the USA in 1980 and ran, on an ex-Lisbon truck, on a short section of tramway in Detroit.

I had the pleasure of a ride on No 14, amongst the skyscrapers of Central Detroit, during a visit in 1982. This book will take you on a very different journey. Instead of skyscrapers, you will start amongst the breweries of Burton and, instead of ending up beside the Detroit River, you will cross the River Trent into Derbyshire passing through small communities of brick terraced houses built around collieries, potteries and other associated industries, with occasional diversions into the fields, and end up in the old market town of Ashby-de-la-Zouch, in Leicestershire.

The trams have long gone; the Midland Red buses which replaced them are now "Arriva serving the North Midlands". The breweries are now fewer but larger, the collieries and most of the associated industries have gone. The brick terraces are still there, but most of the fields are covered by the larger houses of a more affluent society. In place of tram poles, there is now the National Forest, possibly giving future generations a taste of what the area was like before agriculture and industry changed it all. This book shows you what it used to be like.

Peter Swift
Spondon, Derby
February 2000

GEOGRAPHICAL SETTING

The route ran south from the old established brewing town of Burton-on-Trent and climbed onto the southern slope of the Trent Valley. It traversed varied geology, much of it of economic importance locally. These strata included the coal measures, sand and clay of South Derbyshire.

The diagrams are from the original plans and are to the scale of 1 inch to 400 yds(1:14400). The maps are from 1925 and are at 6ins to 1 mile(1:10560).

HISTORICAL BACKGROUND

The Burton & Ashby Light Railways formed an unusual, possibly unique tramway. It was a wholly owned subsidiary of a railway company, the Midland Railway, and appeared to operate in competition to that Company's own railway services between Burton, Swadlincote, Woodville, Ashby-de-la-Zouch and Gresley.

The first attempt to construct a tramway to provide communication between these growing South Derbyshire communities originated in 1899 when a group of tramway promoters, supported by the Midland Railway, applied for a Light Railway Order. An objection by the Corporation of Burton-on-Trent, however, quashed the idea.

The second attempt in 1902 received Burton-on-Trent's support, but this time the Midland Railway changed sides and objected to the potential competition with their own railway services around and through South Derbyshire. The promoters, however, came to terms with the Midland Railway who shortly afterwards applied for their own Light Railway Order. This was almost identical to the one they had objected to, differing only in that the proposed route would pass through the developing township of Newhall. It is almost certain that this diversion prevented an even earlier demise of the system. Newhall was not adjacent to a railway station and so benefited from the tramway more than the other townships of South Derbyshire.

This last proposal received assent and the tramway duly opened in 1906. The estimated cost of construction was £89,926.13s.3d.

The area of Derbyshire served by the tramway had developed industrially rather than commercially and the "Tramway and Light Railway Journal" of 1st June 1906 describes how heavy use of the railways in the area for industrial purposes precluded a passenger service of adequate sufficiency. The industries included many coal mines, clay mines and manufacturers of pottery and heavy clay goods including chimney pots, tiles, drainage pipes, conduits, firebricks and sanitary ware, most of these factories being small and relying on rail transport for the distribution of the major portion of production to all parts of this country and abroad.

Initially three services were operated:

1. Burton-on-Trent to Ashby-de-la-Zouch via Swadlincote from 2nd July 1906.

2. Swadlincote to Gresley Station commenced 24th September 1906, and provided a connection with cars to Burton and to Ashby at The Delph, Swadlincote.

3. Church Gresley (Boot Inn) to Woodhouse Junction, Woodville. It commenced on 15th October 1906 but this service was not a success and ceased in 1912.

The unique tram system closed on the 19th February 1927, just short of its 21st birthday. Telephone Exchange No. 1 was unplugged for the last time and at midnight on the 19th all the miles of bright rails went dead for ever. Ten cars were sold to Tynemouth & District Electric Traction Company and ran a few more miles. Three other survivors are described in caption 117.

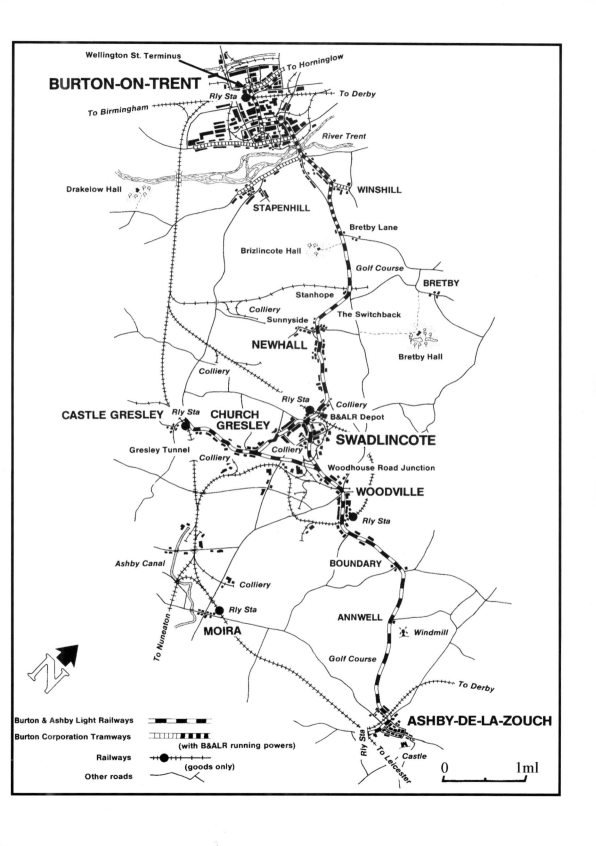

Wellington St. Terminus

BURTON-ON-TRENT

To Horninglow

Rly Sta To Derby

To Birmingham

River Trent

Drakelow Hall

WINSHILL

STAPENHILL

Bretby Lane

Brizlincote Hall

Golf Course

BRETBY

Stanhope

Colliery
Sunnyside

The Switchback

NEWHALL

Bretby Hall

Colliery

Rly Sta

Colliery
B&ALR Depot

CASTLE GRESLEY *Rly Sta* **CHURCH GRESLEY**

SWADLINCOTE

Gresley Tunnel

Colliery

Colliery

Woodhouse Road Junction

WOODVILLE

Rly Sta

Ashby Canal

BOUNDARY

Colliery

ANNWELL

Rly Sta

⚒ *Windmill*

To Nuneaton

MOIRA

Golf Course

To Derby

Rly Sta *Castle*

ASHBY-DE-LA-ZOUCH

To Leicester

Burton & Ashby Light Railways

Burton Corporation Tramways

(with B&ALR running powers)

Railways

(goods only)

Other roads

0   1ml

BURTON-ON-TRENT

1.   Car 11 stands at the terminus in Wellington Street. The trolley pole will be swung and the car will depart for Ashby-de-la-Zouch via Newhall, Swadlincote and Woodville with many rural stops en route. Any reader wishing to visit the area to follow the route will find the alms houses to the left of this picture directly behind car 11. To the right of the illustration, but not in view, on the corner of Borough Road and Wellington Street stands a large shop, now a motorcycle dealer. This was the county stores of Messrs. R.Wilkinson.

2.   Car 10 nears its journey's end from Ashby via Swadlincote. Pictured in Station Street, it will be passing the Midland Railway Station before its arrival at the terminus. Pictures of B&ALR cars in Burton are very rare. The shops, left, comprised those of Ernest Abrahams & Horace Dudley, local photographers. The upper premises were occupied by the Bridge Temperance Hotel. The Temperance was a lonely outpost in a town bristling with breweries and pubs.

Exciting Tram Accident in Burton

CAR KNOCKED OFF THE RAILS.

THE SERVICE DISLOCATED.

On Tuesday evening a serious tram accident which, fortunately, was not attended with any fatal results, was the cause of much excitement prevailing in Station Street.

Shortly after 5.30 a Burton and Ashby Light Railway car was proceeding along Station Street when a horse attached to a heavy dray belonging to Messrs. Bass, Ratcliff, and Gretton, Limited, took fright at the tram-car bell. The animal dashed out of Cross Street at a tremendous pace, and the dray collided with the rear of the passing car (No. 3). with such force as to bodily lift it off the rails. The force of the compact also threw the driver from the car, but, fortunately, he fell clear

or both the tram and the dray, and, consequently, escaped with minor injuries.

A strong band of officials and workmen was quickly on the spot, but despite their energies it was some time before the car could be righted, and the traffic was blocked to such an extent that a procession of no less than twelve cars was formed.

Even when, after about half-an-hour's labour, the car was removed to the Burton Tramway Depot, it was some time before the local service was again put in working order for the demands made on the traction power proved too great, and a number of the cars were compelled to remain stationary while others moved on.

Later in the evening the driver was removed to his home at Newhall, and the damaged car to the Swadlincote depot. The damage to the rear of the car and the dray was rather considerable.

3.   Car 6, bound for Ashby, is pictured passing along Guild Street. The shop on the extreme right of the photograph, J.Simnett, is of particular interest. Mr Simnett toured all of the surrounding vicinity on his cycle using his camera to record events and scenes. It is thanks to his skill and enthusiasm that a wonderful collection of photographs of the area is available today; many are used herein.

4.   Car 13 waits with Midland Railway officials and engineers on Burton's river crossing with a Burton Corporation car held up by the photographer. This is a proving run and the event is being recorded by Mr Simnett and probably an MR photographer. This was the only bridge across the Trent at Burton to carry traffic in and out of town at that time. It replaced an earlier crossing built in the 12th century. This new bridge opened in 1824 and took a straighter route to accommodate a greater traffic volume.

5.   Car 13 again. A superb view of a brand new car, and the same occasion as the previous illustration. The gent on the top deck centre, wearing a pill box cap, is a Burton policeman. The trees beyond outline the Winshill area to which the tram will eventually proceed on its return from Wellington Street Terminus.

6. A Burton & Ashby car (extreme right) in a later LMS livery stands for passenger embarkation on the newly widened section of the bridge. The construction followed the Bearwood Hill disaster of 1919. A Burton Corporation enclosed car (left) trundles towards the town. Two Corporation open top cars were reserved solely for the Bearwood Hill route. After the accident only these and the

	AM	AM	AM	AM	AM	AM	AM	AM	N'n		PM	PM	PM	PM	PM	PM	PM	PM	PM
ASHBY STATION ...d	...	...	8 0	849	9 20	10 0	1040	1120	12 0		...	1240	...	1 20	...	2 0	...	240	...	320
Hill St. Loop. Ashby...	...	...	3 7	847	9 27	10 7	1047	1127	12 7		...	1247	...	1 27	...	2 7	...	247	...	327
Golf Links, Ashby......	...	...	910	850	9 30	1010	1050	1130	1210		...	1250	...	1 30	...	210	...	250	...	330
M'lt Shovel Inn, Answ'll	...	...	812	852	9 32	1012	1052	1132	1212		...	1252	...	1 32	...	212	...	252	...	332
Boundary Chapel	...	...	816	856	9 36	1016	1056	1136	1216		...	1256	...	1 36	...	216	...	256	...	336
Woodville Reservoir ...	...	...	820	9 0	9 40	1020	11 0	1143	1220		...	1 0	...	1 40	...	220	...	3 0	...	340
Station St. Woodville	...	704	822	9 2	9 42	1022	11 2	1142	1222		...	1 2	...	1 42	2 2	222	242	3 2	322	342
Tollgate, Woodville ...	...	707	825	9 5	9 45	1025	11 5	1145	1225		...	1 5	...	1 45	2 5	225	245	3 5	325	345
Woodhouse Road Jnc.	...	707	828	9 9	9 49	1028	11 8	1148	1228		...	1 8	...	1 48	2 8	228	248	3 8	328	348
Swadlincote {......a	...	745	834	914	9 51	1034	1114	1154	1234		...	1 14	...	1 51	214	234	254	314	334	354
Market Place {......d	710	755	835	915	9 55	1035	1115	1155	1235		1255	1 15	135	1 55	215	235	255	315	335	355
Hope & Anch'r Inn, Nh'l	715	8 0	840	920	10 0	1040	1120	12 0	1240		1 0	1 20	140	2 0	220	240	3 0	320	340	4 0
Sunnyside, Newhall ...	723	3 5	845	925	10 5	1045	1125	12 5	1245		1 5	1 25	145	2 5	225	245	3 5	325	345	4 5
Stanpope Bretby	725	813	850	930	1010	1050	1130	1210	1250		1 10	1 30	150	2 10	230	250	310	330	350	410
Burton Golf Club	727	812	852	932	1012	1052	1132	1212	1252		1 12	1 32	152	2 12	232	252	312	332	352	412
Bretby Lane...............	730	815	855	935	1015	1055	1135	1215	1255		1 15	1 35	155	2 15	235	255	315	335	355	415
Winshill, Al'xandra R	735	820	9 0	940	1020	11 0	1140	1220	1 0		1 20	1 40	2 0	2 20	240	3 0	320	340	4 0	420
Swan Hotel, Trent Bdg	742	827	9 7	947	1027	11 7	1147	1227	1 7		1 27	1 47	2 7	2 27	247	3 7	327	347	4 7	427
Burton, Railway Stn.	753	833	913	953	1033	1113	1153	1233	1 13		1 33	1 53	213	2 33	253	313	333	353	413	438
Burton, W'llington St a	753	833	913	953	1033	1113	1153	1233	1 19		1 39	1 59	213	2 39	259	319	339	359	419	439

Ashby ones were allowed access. In the background, middle distance, can be seen a chimney. This marks the site of Boddingtons Brewery. The building was acquired by Mr C.J.Spooner whose firm later became world famous for its production of fairground rides. His name can still be seen on the superb carved horses on preserved carousels, commonly called the gallopers.

PM PM PM	PM PM	PM PM	PM. PM.	PM.	PM.	PM.	PM.	PM. PM. PM. PM.	M	PM. PM.
...4 0 ...	4 0 ...	520	... 6 0	.. 6 40	..	7 20	..	8 0	.. 8 40	9 30	... 1020
4 7 ...	4 17 ...	527	... 6 7	.. 6 47	..	7 27	..	8 7	.. 8 47	9 37	... 1028
4 10 ...	4 50 ...	530	... 6 10	.. 6 50	..	7 30	..	8 10	.. 8 50	9 40	... 1030
4 12 ...	4 52 ...	532	... 6 12	.. 6 52	..	7 32	..	8 12	.. 8 52	9 42	... 1032
4 16 ...	4 56 ...	536	... 6 16	.. 6 56	..	7 36	..	8 16	.. 8 56	9 46	... 1036
... 4 20	5 0 ...	540	... 6 20	.. 7 0	..	7 40	..	8 20	.. 9 0	9 50	... 1040
4 22 ... 4 2	5 2 522 542	6 2 622 6 42 7 2	.. 7 22	.. 7 42	8 2	8 22 8 42 9 2 9 22 9 52 1038 1042
4 5 4 2 4 45	5 5 525 545	5 625 6 45 7 5	.. 7 25	.. 7 45	8 5	8 25 8 45 9 5 9 25 9 55 1041 1045
4 8 4 48 4 47	5 8 528 548	6 8 628 6 48 7 8	.. 7 28	.. 7 48	8 8	8 28 8 48 9 8 9 28 9 58 1044 1048
4 14 4 43 4 53	514 534 554	614 634 6 54 7 14	.. 7 34	.. 7 54	8 14	8 34 8 54 9 14 9 34 10 4 1050 1054
4 15 4 35 4 53	515 535 555	615 635 6 55 7 15	.. 7 35	.. 7 55	8 15	8 35 8 55 9 15 9 35 10 5
4 20 4 40 5 0	520 540 5 0	620 640 7 0 7 20	.. 7 40	8 0	8 20 8 40 9 0 9 20 9 40 1010
4 25 4 45 5 5	525 545 5 5	625 645 7 5 7 25	.. 7 45	8 5	8 25 8 45 9 5 9 25 9 45 1015
4 30 4 50 510	530 550 610	630 650 7 10 7 30	.. 7 50	..	8 30	9 10 9 30 9 50
4 32 4 52 512	532 552 612	632 652 7 12 7 32	.. 7 52	..	8 32	9 12 9 32 9 52
4 35 4 55 515	535 555 615	635 655 7 15 7 35	.. 7 55	..	8 35	9 15 9 35 9 55
4 40 5 0 520	540 6 0 620	640 7 0 7 20 7 40	.. 8 0	..	8 40	9 20 9 40 10 0
4 47 5 7 527	547 6 7 627	647 7 7 7 27 7 47	.. 8 7	..	8 47	9 26 9 47 10 7
4 58 5 18 538	558 618 638	658 718 7 38 7 58	.. 8 18	..	8 58	9 38 9 58 1018
4 59 5 19 539	559 619 639	659 719 7 39 7 59	.. 8 19	..	8 59	9 39 9 59 1019

M Last Car having connection at Swadlincote for Castle Gresley,

7.   A Burton & Ashby car heads towards Winshill. The River Trent looks tranquil at this point but lower downstream, towards Swarkstone and Derby, the flow can be severe. The Roman name "Trisantona", it has been suggested, means "The Trespasser" as it is prone to flooding along its wide plain and has over the years altered its course many times on its way to the sea. Once famed for an abundance of salmon, it was also made navigable up to Burton.

8.　　　Car 20 cautiously approaches the curve of track leading to the Swan Hotel and to the bridge. This view illustrates the severe gradient of Bearwood Hill with Winshill beyond. The sharp curve proved a hazard as will be seen in the next illustration. The provision of two parallel wires meant that overhead points were not required at the passing loops.

9.　　　Car 19 and complete disaster! On Wednesday 8th October 1919 at 11.35am during its ascent of the aforesaid gradient, adhesion was lost. All means of arresting the vehicle were brought into operation, brakes (hand and electrical), slipper, also sanding and panic, but to no avail, the car gained momentum. Conductress Lilian Parker left her duties and descended to the rear platform applying the handbrake at that end, without success. She sadly sustained injuries which later proved fatal. Driver Charles Insley was uninjured but greatly shocked. The car was later righted by Burton Fire Brigade and then driven to Swadlincote Depot.

10.   Car 13 passes the builders yard of E. Wigley. He was also a joiner and sawmill operator. The property later became the Corporation Depot (not tram). The passengers on board for the test run are the aforesaid officials as the tram approaches the midway point of the climb, just past the walled doorway. This would be about the spot 19 had reached prior to its uncontrollable descent. A Board of Trade enquiry proved one reason for poor adhesion was wet and slippery leaves on the track.

WINSHILL

11.   Car 13 is at rest for more photographic records to be made. The crew and officials will continue on a steady gradient along Highbank Road, towards the main road. It became the A50 and is now renumbered A511.

12.   Car no 1 speeds towards its eventual destination with passengers making good use of the upper deck on this summers day. The area to the left and right is now built up. There is industry in this scene evident from the twin chimneys of Messrs. Hodges Brickworks.

13.   Car 9 stops at the crest of Highbank Road to allow a passenger to alight before heading along Ashby Road, now the A511. The solitary building visible in the middle distance is the Waterloo Inn and, for those readers who navigate by pubs, this one is still in use. Beyond is the smokey atmosphere tinged with the aroma of hops of Burton with its many breweries. The open fields on the left are now lined with residential properties, otherwise the road layout remains the same. The telephone wires carried messages to and from the town and were under control of the National Telephone Company, using simple number arrangements and manned exchanges. The tram depot at Swadlincote was National no. 1. All the Burton & Ashby cars carried their own emergency phones in a wooden hinged box and these could be plugged into roadside links. One of these connections can be seen on the right hand tension pole with the cable passing above the centre catenary.

14.   Two Burton & Ashby Cars stand at the junction of Bretby Lane (right) and the A511 and what appears to be trouble. The nearest vehicle has become derailed. This was frequent during and after heavy snowfalls. Compacted snow and ice filled the rail grooves and the frozen mixture built up on the rail surface, lifting the wheels above the rails causing the car to slide away from the track. Derailment was rectified by the crew levering with crowbars. Snowplough attachments were fitted to the tram fenders when severe winter conditions prevailed but obviously were not all that effective. The bleak scene illustrated is probably the blizzard of 1914. The lie of the land on this and the Woodville to Ashby route causes severe drifting and during these times some journeys were abandoned. Passengers near to their destinations walked the rest of the way, whilst others going further sought refuge at the nearest hostelry.

15.   Car 13 is seen at rest once again. To the left of this passing loop is the Stanhope Arms, at this period a simple country pub, as will be seen on the following picture. Today it is much larger and is a restaurant as well. This area is so named because it is close to the village of Bretby and its association with the Stanhope family and Bretby Hall. On the right of Car 13, behind the wall, was Bretby Colliery, now disused but with the winding house remaining. It was connected to the M R Burton to Leicester line by a spur which passed beneath the road. The parapet of the bridge is seen to the rear of the section box. On occasions the line was used to deliver race horses for the Sixth Earl of Chesterfield of Bretby Hall, where he had a training race course. Another visitor who found the siding useful was Benjamin Disraeli, Earl of Beaconsfield, Prime Minister of England. His own private coach would transport him from Burton to the siding.

16.   Car 8 trundles past maintenance staff at work on standard No. 112. It has just passed a Burton bound car at the loop provided here and is about to turn left to enter the reserved section, or as it was called locally "The Cutting". An amusing story relating to this location was told by the late Harold Twells,employed as a conductor two years before the system closed. On nearing the Stanhope stop he would call out Stanup! A large party of travellers new to the area and on their way to Burton were seated in the lower saloon (capacity 22). They all obeyed the instruction and stood up, probably thinking some mechanical fault had occurred. Any locals standing being familar with the announcement alighted at the Inn, leaving the visitors still vertical. Embarrassment resulted for Harold and passengers until all was humorously explained and the journey was resumed.

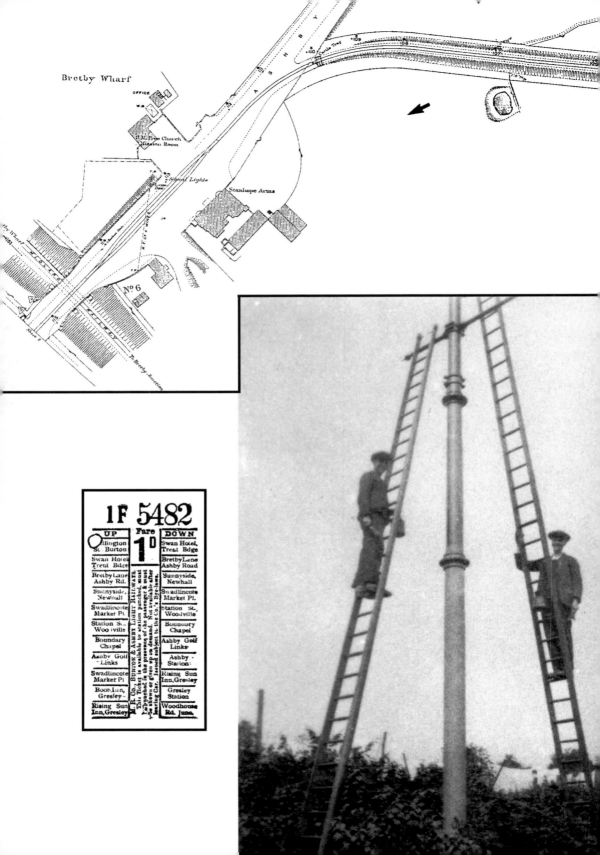

Bretby Wharf

OFFICE
W.R.

P.M. Free Church
Mission Room

Signal Lights

Stanhope Arms

No 6

To Bretby Junction

17.   A closer look at the painters seen in the previous picture shows them applying Midland Lake. Traces of this colour were found on two ornate bases rescued from Newhall streets after serving as sewer vents with slotted apertures in the finials. On closure all other standards were jacked out of the ground from a depth of 6 feet at a rate of six a day, then taken for storage at Woodville Goods Depot ready for sale, most going to Derby Corporation for use on their trolleybus system.

18.   Car 19 waits with a string of five followers in the Stanhope loop. An outing to Brizlincote Hall is the joyful occasion. Sunday School teachers, helpers and children eagerly pose for the camera whilst a line of drivers also get in on the act. They have driven from Church Gresley via Swadlincote. Mr William Barton, Traffic Superintendent, strikes a nonchalant pose by the dash rail attired in Sunday best, complete with straw boater to shade him from the summer sun. Enamel advertisement panels are now displayed to help the Company's revenue, almost all relating to Burton traders. Brizlincote Hall lies between here and Burton.

19.   Car 1 heads for Burton after its swaying journey over the switchback. The open fields beyond are now the site of Bretby Business Park, originally built for mining research under the ownership of the National Coal Board. The lane to the left is the main road to Woodville and Ashby-de-la-Zouch, now the busy A511. Bare trees, dull sky and well clad passengers portray a wintry scene.

20.   Car 13 eases across the cattle grid at the entrance to the reserved section. This much photographed vehicle displays what to some may be an unlucky number choice for the run. I will give the reason: The first batch of cars delivered to Swadlincote Depot were numbered 1 to 13 and the last one, being the newest, was chosen for the test. Another seven eventually arrived giving a fleet of twenty.

21.   Car 12 decelerates on approaching the main road, heading for Burton. The motor cycle in the left foreground belongs to Mr F W Scarratt of Derby and is propped on its stand whilst its owner takes a picture for postcard publication. Notice boards have been installed since the previous picture was taken, one stating "Beware of the Trams" (left) and the other is a trespass warning.

22.	Car 5 coasts along on an autumnal day, with Bretby Colliery clearly visible on the left hand skyline. After its demise it became a sawmill worked by Mr Samual Faulkner and at the time of writing is still in operation by his descendants. Note the plain trackside poles with no ornate bases or wrought iron brackets, no doubt considered unnecessary out in open country.

23.	Car 5 speeds along the downgrade in another excellent view of the cutting and surroundings. The cluster of buildings seen on the skyline is at Stanhope, with the Colliery Branch embankment visible on the extreme left, marked by a lighter tone and topped by hedges. A lane runs alongside connecting the factory of Bretby Brick & Stoneware which manufactured a large variety of clay products, including bricks. The land it occupies has the nickname "Klondyke", derived from the period (1896) when the land was leased to Mr Henry Barnes, the founder of the Works.

24.	Car 6 eases up the gradient. Evidence of earthwork is on the right which, no doubt, gave rise to the local name of this stretch, "The Cutting". This must have been a pleasant run during the summer months.

25.   A reverse view of the previous picture in the early days of 1905 shows single track, sleepered, and laid on ballast ready for the 1906 opening of the system. The Callender Cable Company's men pose for the camera. Yards of feeder conduits are channelled in on the right; they are possibly locally made as several clay manufacturers produced these salt glazed items. The three-way conduits will return 550 volt DC electricity from the rails at intervals.

26.   Car 3 trundles along on a grey overcast day. This photograph was taken by J.E.Rowley of Swadlincote. Another well known photographer of the period was Joseph Perks, each of them producing postcards which thus provided a record for posterity.

27.   The cutting in the grips of winter. Travellers in those days suffered more discomfort than today; no snug cars and buses as now. Heating on the tramcars was non existent and drivers arriving at a terminus would withdraw their hands from their gauntlet gloves which were left frozen to the brass controllers and handbrakes! Perish the thought.

28.   Car 17 wends its way along The Cutting's pleasant landscape. In the left foreground can be seen a neatly prepared allotment, giving a productive pastime to employees of the Burton & Ashby Light Railways.

29.   A straight approach to the next stop. This will be at Sunnyside and the travellers will be entering an area abounding with pubs and off-licences. A haven for the thirsty miner or clay worker ('twas a hard life in those days). The 1912 Town & County Directory lists 21 pubs in Newhall, many conveniently situated on the route.

30.   The pastoral scene will now change for the passengers of the approaching car (right), as it enters this built up area of industrial South Derbyshire. The trolley standards with their elaborate wrought iron tracery and fancy cast bases now replace the utility variety across country. Tram activated signals are visible on No. 82 standard, see map. They indicated up to three cars at any one time between here and the next loop. All one colour and not as today's green amber and red variety, this sytem of signalling was installed by Bracknell, Munro & Rogers. The traction standards were manufactured by James Russell & Sons of Wednesbury.

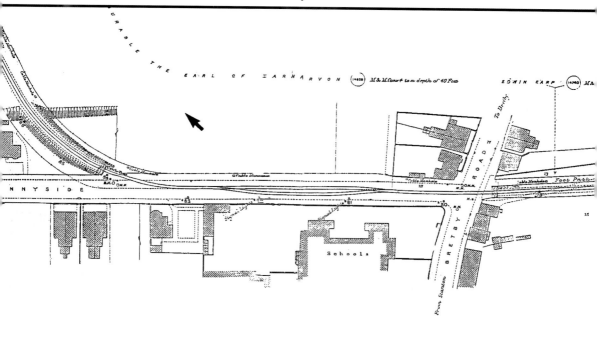

31.   A car grinds around the curve to enter the switchback whilst school children mill around the entrance to the Newhall Council School which is to the left. This road leads to the aforesaid Klondyke Works, beyond the rise.

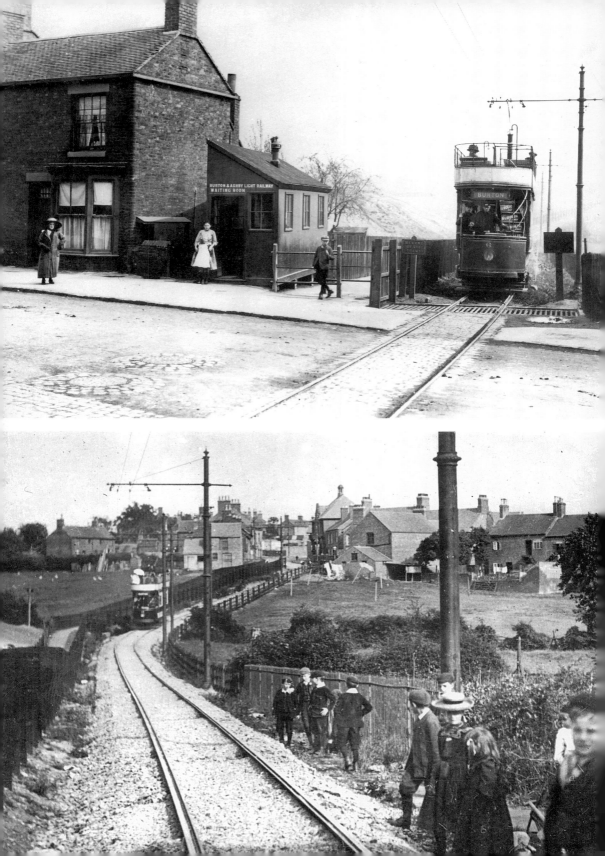

32.   Car 6 passes one of only two waiting rooms on the system, this one having a stove affording comfort during inclement weather. Both were constructed by William Bagnall, a joiner from Ashby-de-la-Zouch and installed a while after the opening of the tramway. Beyond the car is a short section of reserved track with a footpath adjacent. This area is known as Mats Yard, probably a corruption of Matchyard. A colliery was stituated here, the shaft being sunk in 1854. The mine was owned by Messrs. Nadin & Company and was named fittingly Mats Yard Colliery. Two drivers are on the platform of No. 6, one of which is under tuition.

34.   Car 13 halts for yet another commemorative picture. Note the less ornate standard, it being on reserved track.

33.   A car heads towards the stop with the waiting room as shown in the previous picture. A number of youngsters are trespassing on railway property, eager to be in the picture. The reserved track borders a public footpath which was still in use in 2000. The Mats Yard Colliery spoil heap is to the left of the path, although the pit had ceased working by 1888. A disaster occurred along this stretch of line when an unfortunate lady was struck by lightning whilst travelling on the top deck; I believe it was fatal.

35.   Car 13 moves away to continue its running test and appears to have startled the horses who were at ease in the previous picture. The first of the aforementioned public houses appears on the right. There were three in a row, The Stanhope Arms, The Angel and the Holly Bush although the third is not yet in view.

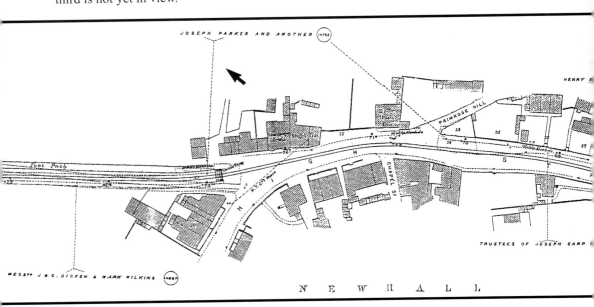

36.   Car 8 makes for the reserved track. The third hostelry is now in view, on the right. Other daily requirements were obtained at the Co-operative Society opposite.

37.　The line wends it way along the High Street passing the "Golden Ball" and "Spread Eagle", then on by the "Royal Oak". Many premises along this stretch were modified to accommodate the track. Newhall was reputedly the result of horse and cart development. Where the horse stopped, the load of bricks was tipped and the house was built.

38.　Car 10 rattles along Union Road to meet up with the High Street, seen in the previous picture. The "Royal Oak" is round the bend in the distance.

39.　A closer look picks out the sign of Henry Harvey Engineer clearly seen on the left. To the right is Warren Bros. boiler manufacturers and engineers, useful firms to have around in an area bristling with collieries and potteries. Warren Bros. were engaged to carry out restoration on tramcar 14, one of three remaining cars found locally. The church tower on the skyline is St. John's and it is here the grave of the unfortunate Conductress Lilian Parker can be found.

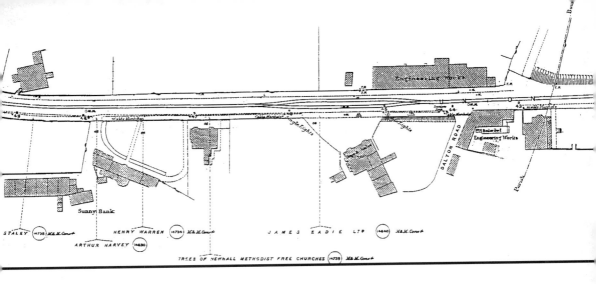

STALEY (4735) M&M.Court

HENRY WARREN (4734) M&M.Court

ARTHUR HARVEY (4430)

JAMES EADIE LTD (4440) M&M.Court

TREES OF NEWHALL METHODIST FREE CHURCHES (4739) M&M.Court

Sunny Bank

40.   Car 11 eases by a horsedrawn load. The rubble seen on the right is a result of road widening necessary for the newly laid track. The premises of Mr Harvey eventually became Warren Bros. thus giving a greater production potential.

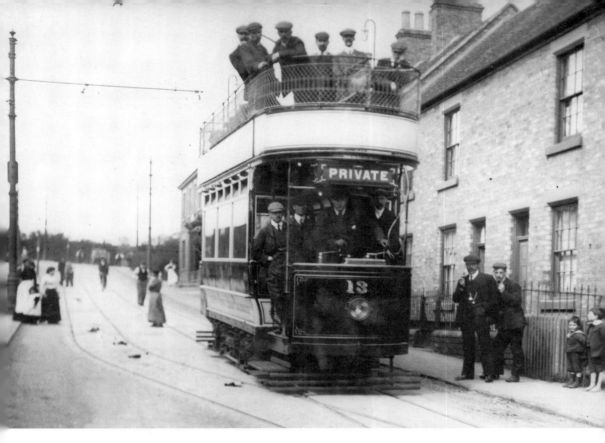

41.   Car 13 slowly makes its way along towards Midland Road signal light (25 on map) where Midland Railway trams and the same company's station and goods depot could be found. A barefoot boy is evident.

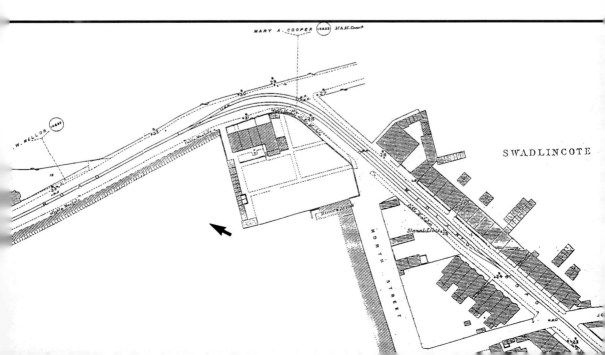

Burton and Ashby Light Railways.
WORKMEN'S CARS.

Early Workmen's Cars will be run as under:—

Bretby Lane	...	...	...	dep.	... a.m.	50
Stanhope Bretby	...	...	...	"	...	6 4
Sunnyside, Newhall	...	...	...	"	...	6 9
Hope & Anchor, Newhall	...	...	...	"	...	6 14
Swadlincote Market Place	...	...	arr.	...	6 19
Do. Do.	...	...	dep.	"	6 20
Woodhouse Road Junction	...	...	"	...	6 24
Toll Gate, Woodville	...	...	"	...	6 27
Station Street, Woodville	...	...	arr.	...	6 29
Station Street, Woodville	...	...	dep.	6 30 a.m.	...
Toll Gate, Woodville	...	...	"	6 32	...
Woodhouse Road Junction	...	...	"	6 35	...
Swadlincote Market Place	...	...	arr.	6 42	...
Swadlincote Car Shed	...	...	dep.	... a.m.	5 40
Hope & Anchor, Newhall	...	...	"	...	5 43
Sunnyside, Newhall	...	...	"	...	5 50
Stanhope Bretby	...	...	"	...	5 54
Bretby Lane	...	...	arr.	...	5 58
Boundary Chapel	...	...	dep.	... a.m.	6 1
Woodville Reservoir	...	...	"	...	6 4
Station Street, Woodville	...	...	"	...	6 7
Toll Gate, Woodville	...	...	"	...	6 12
Woodhouse Road Junction	...	...	"	...	6 13
Swadlincote Market Place	...	...	arr.	...	6 19
Do. Do.	...	...	dep.	"	6 20
Gresley Colliery	...	...	arr.	"	6 29
Gresley Colliery	...	...	dep.	6 30 a.m.	
Swadlincote Market Place	...	...	arr.	6 42	
Swadlincote Market Place	...	...	dep.	... a.m.	5 45
Woodhouse Road Junction	...	...	"	...	5 49
Toll Gate, Woodville	...	...	"	...	5 52
Station Street, Woodville	...	...	"	...	5 55
Woodville Reservoir	...	...	"	...	5 58
Boundary Chapel	...	...	arr.	...	6 0

Workmen travelling to or from work between Bretby Lane, Gresley Colliery, and Boundary Chapel may travel at reduced fares on any cars between the hours of 3.0 p.m. and 6.0 p.m. Mondays to Fridays (both days inclusive) and between 11.0 a.m. and 1.30 p.m. on Saturdays.

42.   Car 9 glides along Midland Road and passes the buildings of Cartwrights Colliery (right). The strange devices hanging from the rear of the vehicle in the foreground are paraffin flares for illuminating market stalls. Looking left, W. Wilkinson's brand new house awaits windows, his wholesale fruit and potato business no doubt financing this.

43.   Car 9 inbound to Swadlincote rumbles over the line to the Cartwright Colliery. The track joined a loop connecting Swadlincote to Woodville. Observe a cycle propped against the overbridge retaining wall. This is the steed of photographer J.S.Simnett. He would have had just enough time to take the previous shot, slip in a fresh plate, swing his tripod and take this second strange exposure. The car depot is centre; three cars await in anticipation of a rush in trade. The centre car is not a steam tram, the tall chimney belongs to the pipe factory of James Woodward, established in 1760. They also made a large range of ornamental garden accessories in terracotta and salt glaze finish. This chimney is the only one left today, a preservation order having been put on it.

44.   Car 11 glides past the depot entrance with the Cartwright Colliery and spoil heap clearly visible centre. It was nicknamed "Shoddy" Pit. The tiny colliery disappeared long ago although one item remains. The office clock still ticks away the hours in the jewellers shop of H.B.Dinnis in Swadlincote High Street. The car sheds and environs remain in use for commercial purposes. They were of sound construction resting on oak piles driven deep into colliery spoil and clay strata. The shed was constructed by the Dick Kerr Company of Preston and not by the Midland Railway.

45.   The Rawlinson Tower Wagon is parked to the left of the depot. The Midland Railway fencing on the right protects the public from the drop to the loop line below. The goods station was situated beyond this. Here thousands of clay products were despatched worldwide, earthquake proof salt glazed pipes being one of the noteworthy items. The overbridge was constructed by Messrs. Tomlinson of Derby using blue engineering bricks.

46.   The Midland Road overbridge was built to carry the trams. Pedestrians at this point had a choice of three means of crossing; by footbridge visible beyond the bridge spans, by road on the lower level and by footpath across the bridge. A modest two platform station lies beyond the latticed footbridge in this picture. The London & North Western goods office is in the left foreground and the Midland Railway goods depot was to the rear of the photographer.

47.   Two of the depot staff take time off to pose for a photograph. Mr Rice, a depot cleaner, is seated in manager Mr James Toulmins' model T Ford. Mr William Lilley, chief mechanical and electrical engineer, leans nonchalantly against the steed. The annual light railway fancy dress dances held at the famous Alexandra Rink were illuminated using Mr Lilly's skill and enterprise.

48. Car 1 (right) displays Midland Railway advertising proclaiming holidays in the Isle of Man via Heysham. This would have been of little interest to most of the locals, being way beyond their financial means. The depot layout, left to right, consists of two four tracked storage bays with room for twenty vehicles, also paint and repair shops. Next is a two storey office block and finally the power house. Snow plough attachments are visible in the left hand foreground.

49.   Car 13 stands ready for the proving run in front of the newly erected sheds. Unballasted track fans out to a single track leading to the gate. These are early days and much tidying up has yet to be done. Greatly modified after the system's closure in February 1927, the building was put to other uses; a drill hall for the Sherwood Foresters T.A., Thompsons Fair during World War II, Messrs. Ericsons munitions factory and later the National Coal Board.

50.   Mr Harold Goodman stands attentively at the controls, having eased the new machine into the daylight in readiness for the official driver to take over; brand new from the Falcon Works of the Brush Company at Loughborough and delivered by rail to Swadlincote Goods Dept, adjacent to its new home; resplendent in Midland Railway crimson lake enhanced by off white rocker panels and decency boards it was finished off with gilt scrolls and lined body panels. The Midland Railway emblem is in the centre.

51.   A north westerly view of the depot complex includes Swadlincote Loop Line laying between the depot and the foreground vegetable plot. Oil storage tanks are situated to the right of the depot yard. Petroleum residual oil was supplied by the Anglo American Oil Company and was delivered by rail in 10-ton tank wagons for use in the power house.

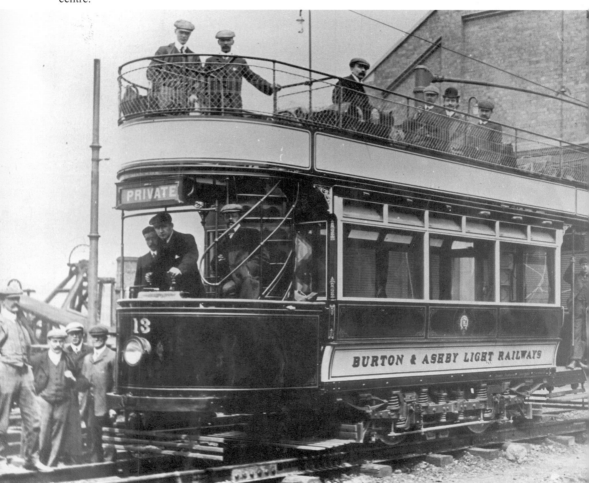

52.   Two Belgian engineers take a break from their work of final checks before the first power surges through the system. They are employees of the Diesel Engine Company of Ghent which supplied the two oil engines. During World War I a hair crack appeared in an engine casing and a replacement was ordered. It never reached England as the vessel carrying the casting was torpedoed by a German submarine, but the engine ran until closure.

53.   The two engines are in evidence in this picture each having three cylinders of 15½ inch diameter by 23 inch stroke and produced 140 bhp. This system of diesel engines charged banks of batteries which evened out load fluctuations. Afternoon services running latterly drew current entirely from the batteries. After closure, many items were sold off, a local plumber and decorator purchasing the glass separators from the batteries to glaze his workshop.

54.   Car 18 rests in the depot yard with step up and collapsible gate across, their correct positions for the driving end. The upper deck lights are clearly visible.

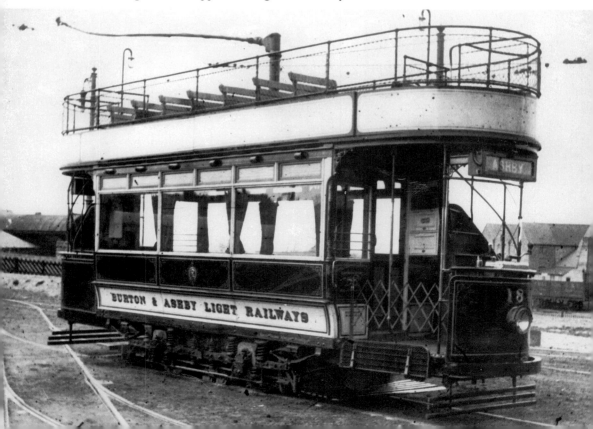

55.   Car 12 accelerates towards the overbridge. The route now heads to the market town of Swadlincote on the right. An early rival of the trams, Messrs Parkes buses had their garage built on the land just to the right of the car. In the distance, on the horizon, the lighter outline of a quarry can be seen. Sand for the driver-operated hoppers located under the lower saloon seats of the trams was purchased from this quarry, and provided better grip on slippery rails. In fact, most of the underseat space contained sand, more weight giving better adhesion. Sand was also used for concealing evidence of sickness brought on by the swaying motion of the cars.

SWADLINCOTE

→

56.   Car 8 stands in Midland Road and the heart of the town, known as the Delph, can be seen just beyond. Two houses dominate the scene. The right hand one is "Bretby Villa" with "Bank House" to the left. Two jardinieres, products of James Woodward's Anchor Works decorate the summit of the steps.

57.   A Burton bound car heads towards Newhall having passed Messrs Buckley's "Homelight" fuel tanker. In the left middle distance is the pottery of S.H.Rowley which specialised in domestic and ornamental pottery, and the Aultcliff Pottery is just beyond. The photograph is taken from the Delph market place. Double track swings left for Church Gresley and right for Woodville and Ashby-de-la-Zouch. Forming a triangle (see map opposite) the layout enabled cars to be turned, a practice rarely employed. Offset trolley masts and some extra long reaches caused dewirements. Austins on the right stocked a good supply of ironmongery.

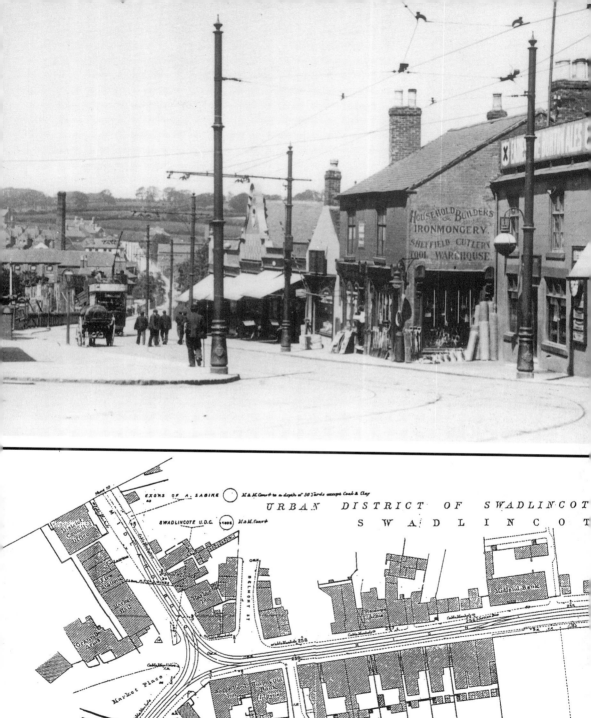

58. Car 3 waits alongside the market hall and we are again looking from the Delph. The hall was erected in 1861 using public subscriptions. The lower building beyond served as Swadlincote's first fire station and the council offices, with gables end on, appear next. The lower structure, last in the row, is the Conservative Club. The market hall also served as the magistrates court.

59. A heavily laden Burton bound car awaits Gresley and Ashby connecting services amidst the market's busy shoppers. The "Granville Arms" is nearby should thirst occur. A pint or two to settle the dust was an expression used by many clay and coal workers. Mr Spittle's butcher's stall is on the right, with the West End Stores just visible on the extreme right.

60.   Car 5 stands outside the "Market Inn" at the Delph, as bandsmen of the Sherwood Foresters Regiment prepair to disembark, the occasion being the death of King Edward VII. Vast crowds assembled in the Delph to mark his passing with a funeral service. The "Nag's Head" is seen in the background.

61.   A new tram bearing the first ornate livery awaits connecting cars at the Delph. Quarter light windows now have company advertising, clear etched lettering on an Oxford blue background.

62.   A whisp of smoke drifts over the valley in the distance as a train leaves Swadlincote Station. The passengers aboard the waiting tram prefer to take a more novel journey to Burton. The conductor chats to Inspector Pickering, nearest to the camera, legs clad in leather gaiters.

63.   Excited Sunday School 'treaters' board the new form of transport, eager to reach the Bath Pleasure Ground at Ashby-de-la-Zouch. They pose before the impressive "Nags Head" Public House. Sunday-best apparel is the order of the day.

64.   Car 16 trundles along Swadlincote High Street; there are not many customers on the top deck. The "Nags Head" is on the right and Woodville and Ashby lie beyond. The tram faces two severe gradients to Woodville.

65.   Hilton's Shop was once the home of Dr Christopher Hall who later moved to a larger house in Church Street. The side door arch has been bricked up and the steps removed for this shop conversion. The fan of overhead wires is justification for including this indifferent photograph of the High Street.

66.   Swadlincote Saturday Market is in full swing; it stayed open late in those days, until ten o'clock at night, paraffin flares providing a homely illumination. Messrs Parkes Central Omnibus creeps into the scene from the right bringing passengers from Church Gresley and Linton via Coppice Side to obtain their weeks supplies. The buses sounded the death knell for the trams; anyone could set up a service to and from wherever they pleased. Some even used flatbed lorries cleaned down and fitted with bench seats.

67.   Car 3 ambles along Swadlincote High Street, Ashby bound on double track. While traction was electric, street lighting continued by gas.

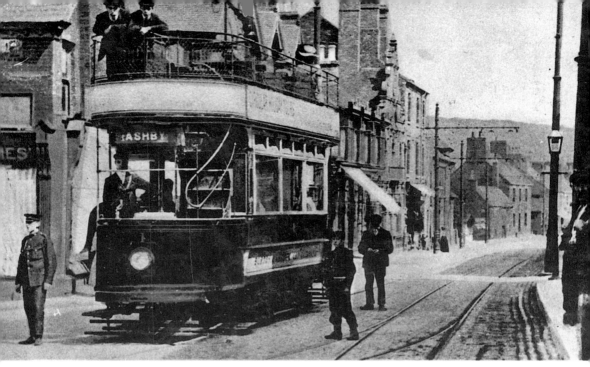

68.   Car 1 stops for another photographer. The crew pose for a moment, no doubt well used to having their pictures taken by now.

69.   The High Street was recorded in the late twenties completely devoid of traffic. Hilton's Shoe Shop (extreme left) has W.Brown next, then Neales Tea Stores sharing this block with J.J.Needham for clothing and Theakers Remnant Stores next door.

70.   Looking back to the Delph area, we see a crossover and ornate catenary standards, with a section box visible below the nearest one. The shop on the left is that of H.B.Dinnis Clockmaker & Jeweller, where the Shoddy Pit Case Clock still marks the passage of time.

71.   Car 13 traverses the High Street in July 1906 and onlookers admire the new form of transport. The large impressive building beyond the car accommodates the Leicestershire Banking Company. Two shacks in the shadow of this are lock-up stalls, one owned by Mr Grice selling fish and chips and the other by Mr A. James famous for his peppermint 'Tommy Dodd' sweets and other mouthwatering confectionery.

72.   A car heads for Woodville, while on the left of Turner & Sons sign is "The Foresters" hostelry, selling Eadies Burton Ales. The clock above the last but one shop is the first premises of H. B. Dinnis who were pawnbrokers as well as clock makers. A steep gradient awaits the car.

73.   Car 1 begins the Hill Street ascent and Mr Bloor's dray, hauled by faithful horse Tommy, heads back to his Woodville Packing Crate Works. The crates will be filled with fragile clay products securely packed with straw. The 1 in 12 gradient ahead was often used for tram brake testing. The 'Pringle' emergency track brake, invented by Mr P.J.Pringle, manager of Burton-on-Trent Corporation Tramways, was tested on this gradient. Photographs of Burton Corporation cars using the Burton & Ashby system have yet to be found, although sightings have been reported by the more mature observers. Beyond the cottages on the left is the Hill Street Baptist Chapel.

74.   Before the ascent of Hill Street, a look can be taken at a scene of live construction of the tramway. Church Street joins Hill Street at this point, a watchman's hut and safety ropes indicating the lines of the route.

75.   Car 7 hauls his passengers onward to Woodville, using its two 25hp motors at maximum output. An open vista of fields appears beyond, looking back to Newhall and Burton-on-Trent. We have now reached one of the main areas of sanitary pipe manufacturers. To the right and to the left especially, was a wilderness of pipe yards belching out clouds of polluting salt smoke. A landscape scarred by huge clay quarries and spoil heaps the scene of desolation added to by many collieries.

76.   A ton of coal, probably from nearby Granville Colliery, is about to be tipped into the road, which is as near to the coalhouse as it ever reached in yesteryear; the customer had to move it! Our eye is led beyond past cycles and carts to the ascending tramcar, on the left of which is seen a gent holding a long pole. Since research suggests all local trams had trolley cords to reverse the arm and not bamboo poles, it can only be assumed that this person is a very late knocker-up.

77.   Car 13 accelerates up the gradient of Swadlincote Road towards Woodville, destination Ashby, on Saturday 20th July 1912. This day is one full of excitement and anticipation for the people in this corner of South Derbyshire. A day away from toil and, for some, a chance to show off their talents. The occasion is the Swadlincote and District Demonstration and Parade, an annual event to raise money for the Nursing Association. The parade followed many sections of the tramway.

WOODVILLE

78.   A car in the later LMS livery enters the toll gate loop, heading for Ashby. The off white rocker panels are now Midland Lake, and the LMS coat of arms embelishes the side panels. On the left is the toll house for the Burton to Leicester turnpike, demolished in the 1930s. The sign above the front porch, at first glance, could be mistaken for an amorial device, but close examination reveals the words 'News of the World'. Between the toll house and the tramcar, just visible, is the second tramway waiting room. This remained in situ until the mid 1950s and was used as a collecting point for the despatch of Sunday newspapers, hence the press advertisement. The ramshackle structure adorned with enamel signs was the garage of Mr Percy Southerns.

79.   A car rests at the tollgate, awaiting customers for Ashby. This is a five-way road junction: see map. The toll house replaced a huge wine cask, originally set up to accommodate a toll keeper. This is why the name 'wooden box' was originally applied to this hamlet. In 1845 the name was changed to Woodville. Queen Adelaide being the instigator of the renaming. In the centre of the scene stands Wooden Box lock up (cooler) or police station. A stone tablet subsequently stolen, proclaimed 'Wooden Box Lock-up'. In the distance is the tall chimney of C.W.Outram, Sanitary Ware Manufacturers.

80.   Cars 2 and 8 pass each other at the toll gate as Mr W.H.Buckley's tanker delivers lamp oil to the "New Inn". Before us stretches the former stage coach route from London to Liverpool, with the *Red Rover* calling at Wooden Box at 8.30am on its way to Ashby, Leicester, Northampton, Dunstable and St. Albans. The Royal Mail coach from Ashby and beyond passed the Wooden Box at 9.30am.

81. Car 5 glides along allowing us a final glimpse of the toll gate junction, the road disappearing ahead to Burton. No. 5 is taking the more lucrative route to the same destination, as the track takes a left hand sweep.

82. We are now looking in the opposite direction from the toll gate and can see the rear end of Mr Buckley's tanker and the name of his fuel. Woodville High Street contained numerous industries on either side and of course the inevitible refreshment houses; six along the next two miles or so, all owned by Brunt Bucknall & Co Ltd of the Hartshorne Brewery.

83. Car 11 plies its route to Burton and a crank axled milkfloat clatters along. Adcocks Newsagency is to the right and a single chimney marks one side of Nadin & Parkers "Reliance" pottery; the rest of the factory was opposite. Further along the High Street on the left was Hartshorne Pottery.

84.   Car 1 stands at the "Joiners Arms" car stop. Passengers may alight here for Woodville Station, approached along Station Street to the right of the car. The station was situated on the Woodville loop, handy for people journeying to Coalville or Leicester. We see that Leicestershire is in contest with Lancashire on the Leicestershire County cricket pitch at the Baths Ground, Ashby-de-la-Zouch.

85.　Car 18 enters the Station Road loop at the "Joiners Arms", a recognised car stop indicated by the sign on the standard. All enamel stop signs were finished in Oxford blue with white letters. Another small brewery owned by Thompsons was once situated to the rear of the Joiners, but this was short lived. To the left is Mr Wright's tent and rope manufactury.

86.　Car 4 passes Woodville water tower, an elaborate structure, its entrance guarded by two charming ornamental lions with a salt glaze finish, probably of local manufacture. The tower provided a good head of water, supplying the Brunt Bucknall Brewery mainly and some domestic users. The tower has gone, along with the brewery although the lions lived on for a time guarding a house built on the site.

87.　　Car 7 glides towards Burton still following the ridge road which is now the A511. The track is still below the surface in 2000, all the way to Ashby-de-la-Zouch Station at an estimated depth of ten to twelve inches below the surface, frequent road works having exposed sections.

88.　　This is our last look at this route until the line descends into Ashby. Not one photograph has come to light beyond the distant house, however a description of the rest of the route is possible. Houses in the above view include Ravenswood and Ivanhoe, with Millfield Street beyond. Then around the bend The Laurels, Huxley Villa and lastly Alton Terrace. Then it is open country until the "Greyhound Inn" is reached, except for the reservoir of Swadlincote and Ashby Joint Waterboard, a recognised car stop. Onwards is the odd cottage to left and right and next is Smistsy toll gate, with good country vistas along the way to the "Red Lion" loop. We are now following the boundary of Leicestershire and Derbyshire. The next pause will be at Anwell Place, near the "Malt Shovel Inn", an official car stop and a good winter refuge for travellers. Trams held up by up to 14ft snowdrifts could only wait overnight for rescue the next day. No hardship for some drinkers!

ASHBY-DE-LA-ZOUCH

89.   Car 11 descends into Ashby on a Summer Sunday with driver Harold Goodman at the helm. White cover for the cap and white gloves is the clue to the day. Having passed the "Malt Shovel" and the ruined windmill, Harold has pressed on to his destination, passing en route Ingleshill Farm (see map), and Ashby Ivanhoe Golf Course (closed 1909). Then it is open undulating country until he reaches Hill Street loop.

0. A car ascends the steep gradient of Burton Road. It is the end of September for in the distance is
showman's steam engine and trailer. The annual Ashby Statutes Fair is now over and they will
egin their slow journey to Burton-on-Trent for their annual function. To the left of the car is the
ignal box for the Midland Railway's Ashby to Melbourne line, which crosses the road at this point.

1. There are also fine dwellings on the other side of the road. The single line track leads down to
Derby Road passing loop. A signal light on standard No. 40 is visible above the gas lamp.

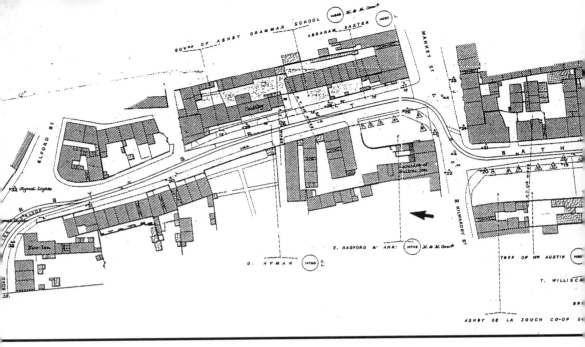

92.	Cars 4 and 12 pass at the Derby Road loop outside The New Inn. Two cars with PRIVATE on the destination blinds is a mystery, yet there are plenty of people getting in on the act. Maybe they are gathering for an outing.

93.   Car 9 negotiates the Derby Road loop heavily laden. A busy scene with hoards of locals out
to, perhaps, witness the first service car in their town. A resident of the "New Inn" props up the pub
yard wall.

94.   Car 3 ambles along Derby Road with, again, plenty of onlookers. Vast changes have occurred
since this picture was taken, with the cottages remaining in 2000 to give a clue to the location.

95.   Car 3 glides along Bath Street. Beyond the trees lies the Royal Hotel and the Bath Grounds, scene of the county cricket matches and many other activities. Dolly Shepherd ascended by balloon and throngs of excited children enjoyed Sunday School outings in its pleasant environs.

96.   A car passes the Loudoun Memorial to Edith, wife of Charles Abney-Hastings. It was designed by Sir George Gilbert Scott and unveiled on 24th July 1879. Ashby's nearby castle is worthy of a visit and is kept well tended. Tram travellers often enjoyed its historic appeal, with a relaxing day and a picnic. The castle's Hastings Tower, although altered by Cromwell, is a link with the long line of the Hastings family.

97.   Car 13, on inaugural duties, eases by the Royal Hotel in Station Road. The objects skyward above the hotel bay are the ears on the overhead wires. Ashby was at one time a spa town, beneficial saline waters being pumped from Moira, some five miles distant. Their subterranean source was discovered during coal extraction. An impressive spa building was situated to the rear of the Royal, with the aforesaid pleasure ground laid out beyond. Sadly, the superb spa building has now been demolished, but it lasted through the tramway period.

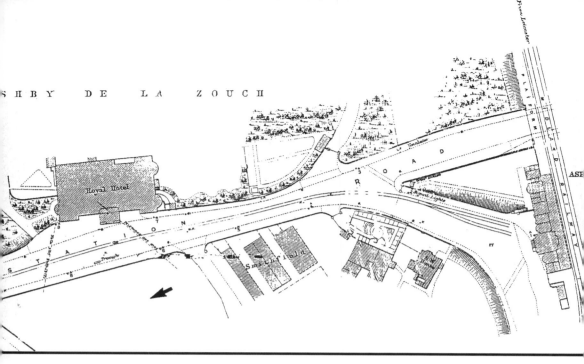

98. Car 11 rumbles past the Royal Hotel, driver Goodman returning it to Burton. In the distanc is the station terminus. The water trough on the pavement remains today and is used for flora displays.

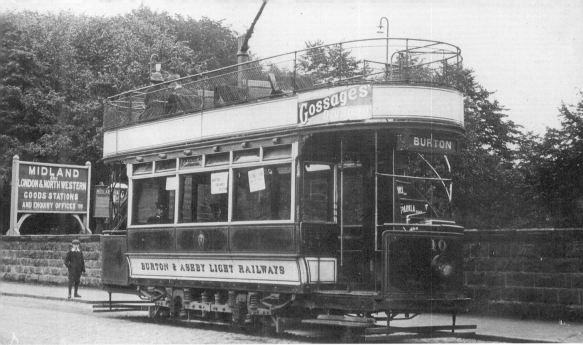

99. Car 10 prepares to pull away from the terminus on the station forecourt. The track and setts can still be observed in 2000 and are in excellent condition. Gaberdine aprons with a Scottish plaid lining were attached to each seat back to protect the front and lap of passengers, affording some degree of comfort. The aprons can be clearly seen in this photograph. A raised brass eye secured the material on the outside seat back and an eyelet looped over a matching brass domed pin on the gangway side. All swingback seats had a three slatted gate fitted below the seat backs suspended by hinges. These gates were anti-pickpocket devices. All ironwork was finished in black and brass fittings were polished.

100. Cars 1 and 13 are at rest on the forecourt of Ashby Station. This occasion was a Board of Trade inspection and a host of children congregated, along with interested adults, to be recorded for posterity. Again the knee covers are clearly seen. The points and double track remain today.

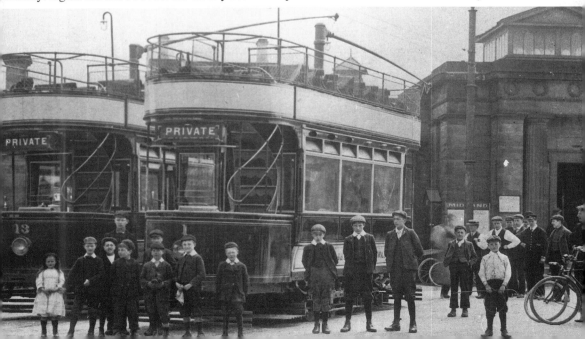

SWADLINCOTE

101. Car 8 trundles along to connect with a waiting car at the Delph. It is arriving from Church Gresley and Castle Gresley and is travelling along West Street. To the right stands the "Bear Inn" between the two taller buildings. Locals have mentioned a trolley pole overhead reverser at this spot, but there is no photographic evidence of this device. Other reports suggested wooden setts in the Delph area, but again there is no evidence.

102. Car 8 is ready to ascend Alexandra Roa leaving West Street to the right and left. Th "British Oak" stands to the right and on the le of the picture is Alfred George Hall's grocer stores. Car 8 now faces the steep gradient o Alexandra Road and it was from this point tha car 19 was tested by Engineer William Lilley afte its 1919 disaster. It was proved mechanicall sound although a press illustration shows variou deck fittings hanging loose and window shattered.

103. Car 13 surges to the summit of Alexandra Road with a clear view of the conductor taking to deck fares. The car stop sign reads ASCENDING CAR STOP ON REQUEST. The firm of R.B.Ha produced postcards at their adjacent printing works, which have been a source of many interestin local tram views. Mr Charles McCann ran the shop on the extreme right and supplied the needs o the music loving population, a phonograph horn being visible in the window. The McCann's were along with other farsighted individuals, instigators of cinematographic entertainment in Swadlincote The 'new fangled moving pictures' had arrived along with the trams.

...andra Road, Swadlincote.

R.B. HALL
PRINTER
AND
BOOKBINDER.
NAT TEL No 577.

CHURCH GRESLEY

104.   Car 20 stands with some sister cars on the occsion of the Gresley Parish Church of St George and St Mary's Sunday School outing on 27th August 1910. Behind the leading car stands Holy Trinity Church, buil for Gresley Parish Church's overspill. The church notice board is visible by the car dash rail. Initially, overloading was rife and conductor Harold Twells boasted an impressive 117 on board from Burton to Gresley Rovers Ground on one occasion.

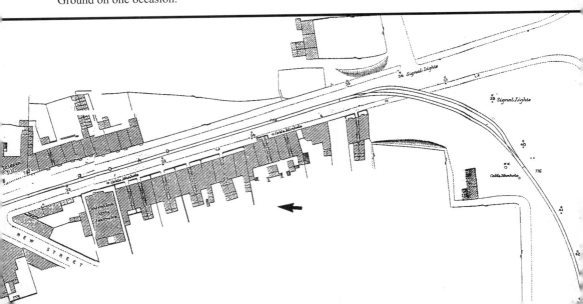

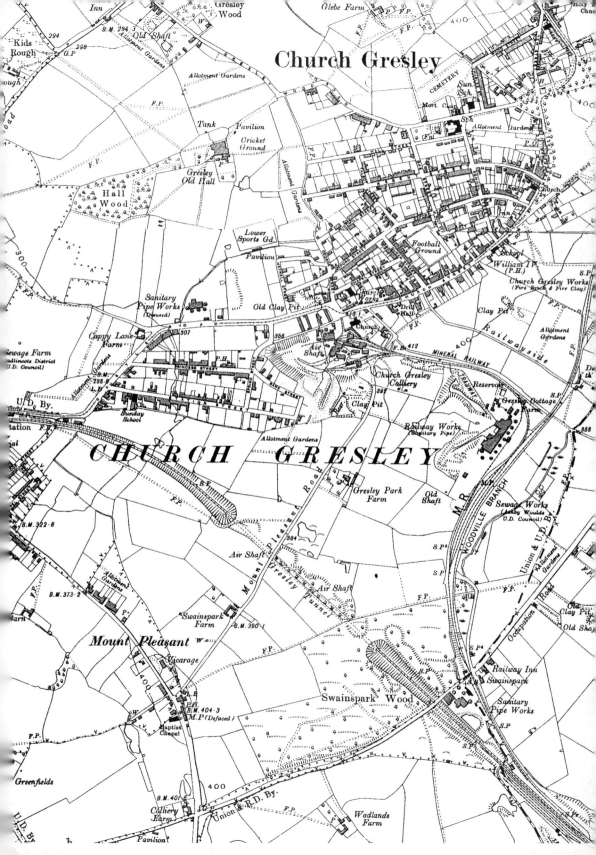

105. Car 20 heads along reserved track on Gresley Common, displaying an exceptionally long trolley arm. All cars had offset masts, the few with long trolley arms combined with the mast position caused accidents to overhanging roofs, removing tiles and gutters on narrow sections. These cars were later banished to the wider Gresley route. The background scene includes the bottle kiln of Sproston & Bostocks Pottery (extreme left) and the chimney of Messrs Thomas Wragg & Sons Coppice Side Pipe Works.

106. Car 20 glides along the broad Market Street - no roof accidents here! The newly landscaped Maurice Lea Memorial Park borders the road on the right which is a welcome restoration to a scarred landscape. On the extreme left is Toft & Waddington's shop, supplying groceries, and beyond (opposite the lamp post) is Gresley Post Office.

107.   Car 6 stands for a photocall further along Market Street. The occasion is the first service car returning from Castle Gresley. The building on the extreme right is the Market Hall which replaced an outdoor market held on a triangle of land opposite. The large ecclesiastical edifice next to the Market Hall is the Primitive Methodist Chapel; the Market Hall later became the Chapel Schoolroom.

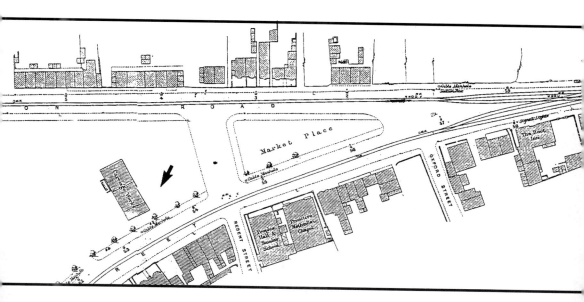

108. Car 12 glides along towards Swadlincote, rattling over a double junction. The twin tracks on the right lead to Woodhouse Junction between Swadlincote and Woodville. Very little used, the service was soon reduced to hourly. It was further cut back to Saturdays only and withdrawn in 1912. The last cars to run on it took the Salvation Army Sunday School treat to Ashby. This intersection was always referred to as The Boot Inn Junction. An obvious choice as we see Worthingtons Burton Ales advertised at this popular ale house. The long low building (right), at this period, was the workshop of Mr S. Grisetti, carriage builder and wheelright. On his departure to Swadlincote it became the Princess Theatre.

109. A south westerly view of the Boot Inn Junction includes the Gresley lock-up, with the fire station adjacent. The lock-up became an incinerator, hence the chimney, but it was eventually demolished. The end-on building was the Dame School.

110.   Another view of the Boot Inn double junction is the last photograph before Gresley Station terminus is reached. Not a single photograph has turned up with a tram visible between these two points. However, the car in the picture will pass, in order, the "William the Fourth", Gresley Rovers Football Ground (on the left in those days), the "Rising Sun", Gresley Colliery and Gresley Church and then a sharp corner was followed by the steep descent of Cappy Hill to Station Street.

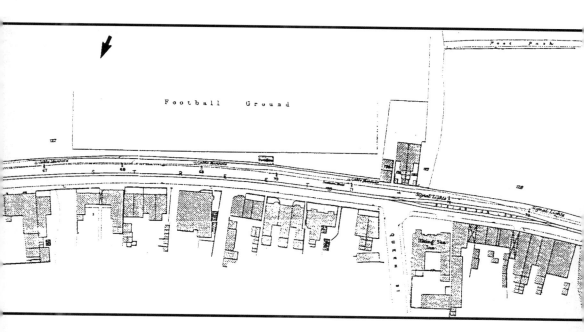

CASTLE GRESLEY

111.   Car 19 is at rest at the Castle Gresley terminus, near the railway station. It stands right in the centre of today's A444. To the left, some four miles distant, lies the village of Netherseal, the final resting place of Sir Nigel Gresley, a man with a great railway distinction. His humble grave may be seen in a small cemetary opposite the village church, where his father was once Rector.

1	3	5	7	2	
1748			Price **2/-**		
MIDLAND, BURTON & ASHBY LIGHT RY.					
Workpeople's					
WEEKLY TICKET					
M	ALEXANDRA ROAD	&	BROOKFIELD & OUT MARKET PLACE	M	
T	BRETBY LANE	&	WINSHOUSE & BIRD JUNCTION	T	
W	STANHOPE BRETBY	&	WINSHOUSE RAMSHOLE	W	
Th	SWADLINCOTE NEWHALL	&	BIRCHMORE CLARE	Th	
F	BRETBY LANE	&	GREEN LANE COLLIERY	F	
S	BOUNDARY DARTS	&	OVERSEX COLLIERY	S	
4				6	

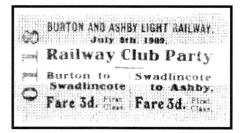

BURTON AND ASHBY LIGHT RAILWAY.
July 8th, 1909.
Railway Club Party
Burton to | Swadlincote
Swadlincote | to Ashby.
Fare 3d. First Class. | **Fare 3d.** First Class.

CASTLE GRESLEY AND CHURCH GRESLEY.
MONDAYS TO FRIDAYS.

	AM	AM	AM	AM		AM	PM	PM	PM
...ESLEY STATION d	8 13	9 8	9 43	10 23	..	11 8	11 43	12 23	1 8
...ing Sun Inn, Q. St.	8 19	9 14	9 54	10 34	..	11 14	11 54	12 34	1 14
...adlincote Mkt Pl. a	8 30	9 25	10 5	10 45	..	11 25	12 5	12 45	1 25

	PM	PM		PM	PM		PM	PM		PM
...ESLEY STATION d	1 48	2 28	..	3 8	3 43	..	4 23	5 8	..	5 48
...ing Sun Inn, Q. St.	1 54	2 34	..	3 14	3 54	..	4 34	5 14	..	5 54
...adlincote Mkt Pl. a	2 5	2 45	..	3 25	4 5	..	4 45	5 25	..	6 5

	PM	PM		PM	PM	PM	PM	PM
...ESLEY STATION d	6 28	7 8	..	7 48	8 28	8 9	4 3	10 23
...ing Sun Inn, Q. St.	6 34	7 14	..	7 54	8 34	9 14	9 54	10 34
...adlincote Mkt Pl. a	6 45	7 25	..	8 5	8 45	9 25	10 5	10 45

SATURDAYS.

...ESLEY STATION d	Before this Car the		PM
...sing Sun Inn, Q. St.	Service is the same		1 28
...adlincote Mkt Pl. a	as Mons. to Fris		1 34
	Time Table.		1 45

	PM		PM		PM
...ESLEY STATION d	1 48	..	2 9	2 28	.. 2 43
...sing Sun Inn, Q. St.	1 54	..	2 14	34	.. 2 54
...adlincote Mkt Pl. a	2 5	..	2 25	2 45	.. 3 5

	PM	PM		PM		PM	PM
...ESLEY STATION d	3 8	3 28	..	3 48	..	4 8	4 28
...sing Sun Inn, Q. St.	3 14	3 34	..	3 54	..	4 14	4 34
...adlincote Mkt Pl. a	3 25	3 45	..	4 5	..	4 25	4 45

	PM			PM
...ESLEY STATION d	4 48	Between these times		1028
...sing Sun Inn, Q. St.	4 54	Cars run more frequently according to		1034
...adlincote Mkt Pl. a	5 5	Traffic requirements		1045

		PM		PM		PM
...ESLEY STATION d	..	1043	..	11 8	..	1128
...sing Sun Inn, Q. St.	..	1054	..	1114	..	1134
...adlincote Mkt Pl. a	..	11 5	..	1125	..	1145

SUNDAY TRAINS.

	PM		PM
GRESLEY STATION d	1 48	Between these times the	8 28
Rising Sun Inn, Q. St.	1 54	Service is the same as	8 34
Swadlincote Mkt Pl. a	2 5	Mons. to Fris.	8 45

	PM		PM		PM
GRESLEY STATION d	9 8		9 48	..	1028
Rising Sun Inn, Q. St.	9 14		9 54	..	1034
Swadlincote Mkt Pl. a	9 25		10 5	..	1045

Q Last Car having connection at Swadlincote for Ashby.
R Last Car having connection at Swadlincote for Burton

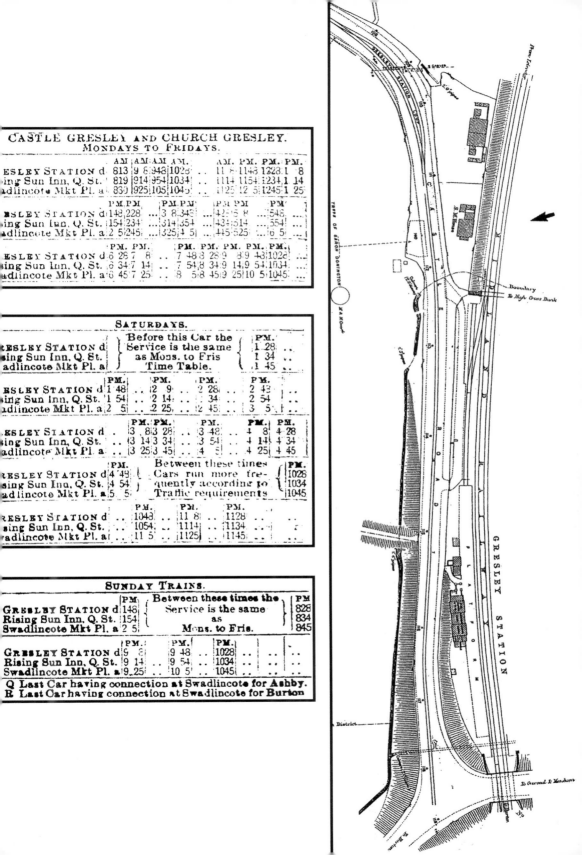

STAFF

112.   The drivers had a dark navy serge uniform wit red piping on the jacket collar and cuffs, also leathe reinforcing bands on the cuffs. The trousers had re piping along the outer seams and highly polished blac boots completed the outfit. The cap insignia comprise the Midland Railway Company Wyvern crest and th company's initials. Collar decoration was also B&AL plus the driver's number.

113.   A Midland Railway telegraphic despatch date 3.55pm on 2nd July 1906 from James Toulmi manager, read: "Opened for traffic successfully th morning. There were no flags or bunting, no brass ban and no official dignitaries, local or otherwise, to giv this glorious new form of local transport a send off. was undoubtedly greatly appreciated by the residen of this corner of South Derbyshire that they ha acquired a superb form of transport which needed n fanfares". Local sales of horses and cycles no dou declined. The official Midland Railway photograph wa taken some time after the opening.

4. The conductress uniform was produced using the ~~me~~ material and in the same colour as the male ~~rsion~~. The chain attached to her jacket lapel holds a ~~gnal~~ whistle with the B&ALR letters and the title ~~he~~ Thunderer" engraved on its side. Also suspended, ~~ong~~ with the whistle, is a telephone box key, oblong ~~shape~~ with an angled taper at its extremity.

115. It is now the London Midland & Scottish Railway period and so the cap has the letters LMS above the peak. An excellent picture for it also shows the cash satchel, whistle, phone key and ticket punch. It is a Sunday and so there is a white cap cover.

ROLLING STOCK

Built by the Brush Electric Car Company of Loughborough, the cars were delivered in tw[o] batches. Numbers 1-13 were followed by 14-20 although provision for 24 cars was made during th[e] car sheds construction. Nos 14-20 were slightly different to the first thirteen delivered. These seve[n] had lockers under the stairs and no saloon window on the nearside front bulkhead. The rheost[at] chamber was located on the platforms, seating capacity being 22 in the saloon and 35 on the to[p] deck.

Dimensions were overall length 28ft/8.5m, height to top rail 15ft 5ins/4.6m, width 6ft 3in[s] 1905mm at pillars and a 6ft/1828mm wheelbase between axle centres. Two 25hp electric moto[rs] propelled each vehicle. Three braking systems were installed: electro-magnetic track brakes, ru[n] back brakes and hand track brakes, a blessing with 1 in 12 gradients or steeper. Track gauge was 3[ft] 6ins/1065mm.

The interior was equally impressive. The ceiling was adorned with lincrusta panels, punche[d] birch veneer, lateral seating, ornate window, bulkhead and door mouldings and cut glass light globe[s] of which there were four in all, to suit the entire lighting circuit of 550 volts DC. Dark maroo[n] curtains clipped back to the saloon window pillars completed the luxury effect.

116.   Car 14 was simply a typical example, but was destined to achieve international fame. Conducto[r] Leonard James is at the controls with driver Charles Wells standing at ease. Harold James emigrate[d] to America, residing in the Detroit area.

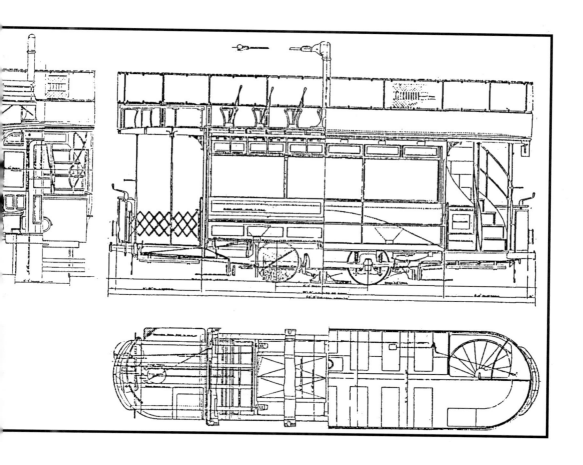

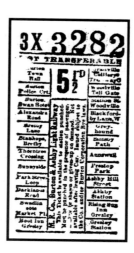

117.   The saloon of car 14 was found at Messrs Whitaker, builders of Church Gresley in 1968, an was removed from their site to Park Road, Church Gresley in September 1970, along with saloo interior fittings from cars 6 and 15 also on the site. Over the next four years 14's saloon was refitte completely and platforms and dash rails added. In 1974 all work ceased due to lack of finance. I 1978 an American company contacted the custodians of 14 offering finance to complete its restoratio to enable it to run on new track in Detroit, between Cobo Hall and the New Renaissance Centre. Th car was removed from Park Road in December 1978 to Warren Bros of Newhall, where, durin 1979, most of its restoration was carried out.

118.   I acquired the last remaining B&ALI motorman's uniform; it had belonged to drive Richard Shipton; the tunic was preserved i excellent condition, there being only slight wea on the collar. The trousers had never been wor from the day they were issued. The whistle an chain were in the right hand tunic pocket alon with a Wyvern cap crest.

19.   Car 14 waits patiently at Warren Bros of Newhall and Don Shuttleworth ambles by after nloading had been completed. Don together with other skilled engineers began the task of completing e saloon, with hired local joiner, the late Mike Sharp, employing his excellent skills with timber.

20.   Car 14 shows it paces on the Detroit Citizens Railway in 1980. One of the first passengers as Presidential Candidate Ronald Regan. From tennis pavilion to a gleaming treasure. The amateurs t Gresley saw the job through and did not waver. The motto of the Gresley Club is *Nil Desperandum* Never say die".

Middleton Press

Easebourne Lane, Midhurst, W Sussex. GU29 9AZ Tel: 01730 813169 Fax: 01730 812601
*If books are not available from your local transport stockist, order direct with cheque,
Visa or Mastercard, post free UK.*

BRANCH LINES
Branch Line to Allhallows
Branch Line to Alton
Branch Lines around Ascot
Branch Line to Ashburton
Branch Lines around Bodmin
Branch Line to Bude
Branch Lines around Canterbury
Branch Lines around Chard & Yeovil
Branch Lines around Cromer
Branch Lines to East Grinstead
Branch Lines of East London
Branch Lines to Effingham Junction
Branch Lines around Exmouth
Branch Line to Fairford
Branch Lines around Gosport
Branch Line to Hawkhurst
Branch Lines to Horsham
Branch Lines around Huntingdon
Branch Line to Ilfracombe
Branch Line to Kingswear
Branch Lines to Launceston & Princetown
Branch Lines to Longmoor
Branch Line to Looe
Branch Line to Lyme Regis
Branch Lines around March
Branch Lines around Midhurst
Branch Line to Minehead
Branch Lines around Moretonhampstead
Branch Line to Padstow
Branch Lines around Plymouth
Branch Lines to Seaton and Sidmouth
Branch Line to Selsey
Branch Lines around Sheerness
Branch Line to Shrewsbury
Branch Line to Swanage *updated*
Branch Line to Tenterden
Branch Lines to Torrington
Branch Lines to Tunbridge Wells
Branch Line to Upwell
Branch Lines of West London
Branch Lines around Weymouth
Branch Lines around Wisbech

NARROW GAUGE BRANCH LINES
Branch Line to Lynton
Branch Lines around Portmadoc 1923-46
Branch Lines around Porthmadog 1954-94
Branch Line to Southwold
Kent Narrow Gauge
Two-Foot Gauge Survivors
Romneyrail
Southern France Narrow Gauge
Vivarais Narrow Gauge

SOUTH COAST RAILWAYS
Ashford to Dover
Bournemouth to Weymouth
Brighton to Eastbourne
Brighton to Worthing
Dover to Ramsgate
Eastbourne to Hastings
Hastings to Ashford
Portsmouth to Southampton
Southampton to Bournemouth

SOUTHERN MAIN LINES
Basingstoke to Salisbury
Bromley South to Rochester
Crawley to Littlehampton
Dartford to Sittingbourne
East Croydon to Three Bridges
Epsom to Horsham
Exeter to Barnstaple
Exeter to Tavistock
Faversham to Dover

London Bridge to East Croydon
Orpington to Tonbridge
Tonbridge to Hastings
Salisbury to Yeovil
Swanley to Ashford
Tavistock to Plymouth
Victoria to East Croydon
Waterloo to Windsor
Waterloo to Woking
Woking to Portsmouth
Woking to Southampton
Yeovil to Exeter

EASTERN MAIN LINES
Fenchurch Street to Barking
Ipswich to Saxmundham
Liverpool Street to Ilford

WESTERN MAIN LINES
Ealing to Slough
Ely to Kings Lynn
Exeter to Newton Abbot
Paddington to Ealing

COUNTRY RAILWAY ROUTES
Andover to Southampton
Bath Green Park to Bristol
Bath to Evercreech Junction
Bournemouth to Evercreech Jn.
Cheltenham to Andover
Croydon to East Grinstead
Didcot to Winchester
East Kent Light Railway
Fareham to Salisbury
Frome to Bristol
Guildford to Redhill
Porthmadog to Blaenau
Reading to Basingstoke
Reading to Guildford
Redhill to Ashford
Salisbury to Westbury
Stratford upon Avon to Cheltenham
Strood to Paddock Wood
Taunton to Barnstaple
Wenford Bridge to Fowey
Westbury to Bath
Woking to Alton
Yeovil to Dorchester

GREAT RAILWAY ERAS
Ashford from Steam to Eurostar
Clapham Junction 50 years of change
Festiniog in the Fifties
Festiniog in the Sixties
Isle of Wight Lines 50 years of change
Railways to Victory 1944-46
SECR Centenary album
Talyllyn 50 years of change
Yeovil 50 years of change

LONDON SUBURBAN RAILWAYS
Caterham and Tattenham Corner
Charing Cross to Dartford
Clapham Jn. to Beckenham Jn.
Crystal Palace (HL) & Catford Loop
East London Line
Finsbury Park to Alexandra Palace
Kingston and Hounslow Loops
Lewisham to Dartford
Lines around Wimbledon
London Bridge to Addiscombe
Mitcham Junction Lines
North London Line
South London Line
West Croydon to Epsom
West London Line

Willesden Junction to Richmond
Wimbledon to Epsom

STEAMING THROUGH
Steaming through Cornwall
Steaming through the Isle of Wight
Steaming through Kent
Steaming through West Hants
Steaming through West Sussex

TRAMWAY CLASSICS
Aldgate & Stepney Tramways
Barnet & Finchley Tramways
Bath Tramways
Bournemouth & Poole Tramways
Brighton's Tramways
Burton & Ashby Tramways
Camberwell & W.Norwood Tramways
Clapham & Streatham Tramways
Croydon's Tramways
Dover's Tramways
East Ham & West Ham Tramways
Edgware and Willesden Tramways
Eltham & Woolwich Tramways
Embankment & Waterloo Tramways
Enfield & Wood Green Tramways
Exeter & Taunton Tramways
Greenwich & Dartford Tramways
Hammersmith & Hounslow Tramways
Hampstead & Highgate Tramways
Hastings Tramways
Holborn & Finsbury Tramways
Ilford & Barking Tramways
Kingston & Wimbledon Tramways
Lewisham & Catford Tramways
Liverpool Tramways 1. Eastern Routes
Liverpool Tramways 2. Southern Routes
Liverpool Tramways 3. Northern Routes
Maidstone & Chatham Tramways
North Kent Tramways
Norwich Tramways
Portsmouth's Tramways
Reading Tramways
Seaton & Eastbourne Tramways
Shepherds Bush & Uxbridge Tramways
Southampton Tramways
Southend-on-sea Tramways
Southwark & Deptford Tramways
Stamford Hill Tramways
Twickenham & Kingston Tramways
Victoria & Lambeth Tramways
Waltham Cross & Edmonton Tramways
Walthamstow & Leyton Tramways
Wandsworth & Battersea Tramways

TROLLEYBUS CLASSICS
Croydon Trolleybuses
Bournemouth Trolleybuses
Hastings Trolleybuses
Maidstone Trolleybuses
Reading Trolleybuses
Woolwich & Dartford Trolleybuses

WATERWAY ALBUMS
Kent and East Sussex Waterways
London to Portsmouth Waterway
West Sussex Waterways

MILITARY BOOKS
Battle over Portsmouth
Battle over Sussex 1940
Blitz over Sussex 1941-42
Bombers over Sussex 1943-45
Bognor at War
Military Defence of West Sussex
Secret Sussex Resistance
Sussex Home Guard

OTHER RAILWAY BOOKS
Garraway Father & Son
Index to all Middleton Press stations
Industrial Railways of the South-East
South Eastern & Chatham Railway
London Chatham & Dover Railway
War on the Line (SR 1939-45)